QUEENS

Don't Settle

A Book of Poems To Empower Women

Desh Dixon

ISBN 10: **1541243749**
ISBN-13: **978-1541243743**

DEDICATION

This book is for all of my Queens around the world. We are Queens ladies.
I salute you. It is my hope and intention that you are encouraged, inspired
and empowered to acknowledge the Queen in you and wear your crown
proudly. Take your power back. Own your Queenness, your highness.

CONTENTS

CONTENTS

ACKNOWLEDGMENTS

I would like to thank all of my fans and supporters around the world for loving me and supporting me as my authentic self. I would like to thank my true friends and family for their unconditional love and support. I want to acknowledge my Queens out there who truly embody the Queendom of uplifting their fellow Queen. Thank you for showing the world that women can collaborate and win together. I love you.

YOUR CHOICE: KEEP SETTLING
OR QUEEN UP

Ladies, it's time to take your rightful place back upon your throne. No matter what you've been through or any past mistakes, you are still a beautiful child of God. You have always been regal. You are a Queen. Queens are royalty. You've been giving away your power for too long. It's time to take your power back. You are worthy and deserving of all your hearts desires.

1 QUEENDOM TIP

Don't shrink for anyone! You are a Queen. No one can denounce your title but you. Shine bright in all your magnificence.

Be Unapologetic

Queen, be unapologetic

You are fabulous, royalty at its best

Be proud of all that you have accomplished

Don't let the Queenless come at you with their mess.

Don't downplay any of your gifts and talents

These are God's blessings, give them the life they need

There is someone who needs you to keep going

To inspire them whoever that may be.

Don't shrink, you're way too eclectic

Don't minimize who you are to fit in

There will always be people who don't like you

Brush them off, keep your confidence from within.

Keep your standards, a Queen must have boundaries

She knows she is a diamond, she is rare

She knows she deserves only the best quality

With her presence, people can't help but stop and stare.

Queen, you do not have to apologize

For your looks, your success or even your size

Reign in your Queendom unapologetically

Forget the naysayers and fabulously continue to rise.

1 QUEENDOM REFLECTION

Think about a time when you felt you couldn't be yourself and had to minimize who you are. How did that make you feel? Do you believe shrinking is helping you maximize your life or minimize it? Marianne Williamson mentions that there's nothing enlightened about shrinking so that other people won't feel insecure around you. Be Unapologetic! What are some things you can do to live bigger as your authentic self?

_____

_____

_____

_____

_____

_____

_____

_____

2 QUEENDOM TIP

Queen, your weight or size has nothing to do with your highness. Don't let society make you think you're less than because of your outward appearance. You're still royalty.

A Queen's Beauty

I know that you may think

That you're ugly because of your weight

You feel it has to be something

Because no one has asked you on a date.

Society tries to define beauty

In a very superficial way

But beauty comes in all shapes and sizes

No matter what society may say.

A Queen is just as pretty

Being a size fourteen or a size ten

Her royalty is not diminished

Her Queenness does not end.

You're perfect here and right now

There is nothing you need to change

You're a magnificent creation of God

You are top level, you are A grade.

So Queen, do not be mistaken

Your highness is always in effect

Regardless of your outward appearance

You're a Queen, demand your respect.

2 QUEENDOM REFLECTION

We live in a society where women have always been held to certain beauty standards based on physical appearance. There's a quote that says 'no one can make you feel inferior without your consent.' You have to love yourself no matter how big or small you are. Love what you see in the mirror. Your weight does not equate to the size of your heart. You're always a beauty! Write down some positive affirmations to say to yourself out loud when you look in the mirror. Ex: I love myself, I am fabulous, I'm so talented, I'm unique, etc.

_____
_____
_____
_____
_____
_____
_____
_____

3 QUEENDOM TIP

Stay true to yourself. Don't try to fit in. Stop seeking approval from others and be your authentic self.

Authentic

The world may try to tell you

That you're supposed to do things a certain way

They try to make you become someone you're not

With lies about how you really get paid.

And when you see some successful people

Who don't have an education or a typical look

You sit back and wonder to yourself sometimes

How in the heck did that person get booked?

See Queen, I'm here to tell you

Your degrees and fancy titles is not what it's all about

One reason you may not be successful

Is because you don't believe in yourself, you have too much doubt.

Authenticity is the new sexy

Being yourself is what the world needs

The gifts and talents that you have to share

Are significant, no matter how small they may seem.

Queen, stay true to yourself

Stand victorious amidst any hate

Do not let anyone derail you

Only you are responsible for the world you create.

Queen, you are authentic

Remember your crown in all that you do

Remember you are a masterpiece from God

You are the best at being you.

3 QUEENDOM REFLECTION

Be yourself. Be your authentic self. Stop trying to please others. There's a saying that one sure way to failure is trying to please everyone. It's impossible. The right people will love you as you are. They need you as you are, not an imitation. How do you show up in the world as your authentic self? If you don't, what needs to change in your life for you to do so?

_____
_____
_____
_____
_____
_____
_____
_____

4 QUEENDOM TIP

You are a Queen. You can rise above anything. No weapon formed against you shall prosper.

<u>Rise</u>

A Queen is a woman of honor

She is regal and full of class

Her royalty comes with its privileges

There is no limit to the wealth she can amass.

So Queen, you can imagine

That you have haters who want you to fail

They secretly hope for your demise

But God won't allow them to prevail.

Do not try to change who you are

Don't stop shining to make others feel good

No weapon formed against you shall prosper

Just accept that you will be misunderstood.

You see, Queenness comes at a cost

That's why some women aren't owning their crowns

The hate, the jealousy, the envy

It's enough to tear some women completely down.

But Queen, do not be discouraged

You are worth it, you're a priceless prize

Forget those who have ill-will towards you

Ascend to your Queendom and continue to rise.

4 QUEENDOM REFLECTION

Queen, stand in your magnificence. No one can take away what God has for you. Even when things don't go as planned, know that you can rise above anything. We all have ups and downs in life. You are a victor, never a victim. What are some affirmations that you are going to say to yourself to declare your victory?

----

5 QUEENDOM TIP

You are worthy and deserving of the best. Don't allow yourself to be taken for granted. You are a priceless jewel. Don't forget that.

Queen You Are

Have you ever stopped

To look and see

At your glowing reflection

Of perfect beauty.

The way you walk

With style and grace

Your flawless hairdo

That goes perfectly with your face.

The stunning heels that make a man melt

He can't help but to come after you

From your perfume that he smells.

Ew ladies, yes ladies, we are Queens

If you didn't know

So there's no such thing as settling

For some ol' low down average Joe.

We are Queens, I say again

We are regal in every way

No matter your past mistakes

That crown from God is here to stay.

So stand tall in your magnificence

Embrace your flaws, imperfections and scars

You are a beautiful creation of God

Be proud of your royalty, the Queen that you are.

5 QUEENDOM REFLECTION

You are priceless Queen. You are to be handled with care. You do not have to decrease who you are or allow yourself to be anyone's doormat. Embrace the full beauty of God's creation that you are. Admire the reflection in the mirror. What are some things you can do to show yourself love?

_____

_____

_____

_____

_____

_____

_____

_____

6 QUEENDOM TIP

Embrace your flaws and imperfections. Stop trying to be perfect. You are perfectly unique as you are. Love and accept yourself.

Love Yourself

Queen, love yourself like no other

You are regal and worthy of praise

You are beautiful with your flaws and imperfections

You are talented in many different ways.

Your size is not of importance

Your curves are perfect as they are

Admire your reflection in the mirror

What you're seeing is the image of a star.

Go out and enjoy some adventure

Go travel the world and have fun

Enjoy the luxury of your own company

And then think about having a special someone.

Take time for all of your hobbies

Do whatever the heck that you please

Make sure that your cup is overflowing

Love yourself to the highest degree.

Queen, love yourself like no other

Your happiness is first, never last

Give more to yourself in abundance

And watch all the wealth you'll amass.

6 QUEENDOM REFLECTION

Love yourself as the Queen you are. You are perfect as you are right here right now. No one else in the world has your fingerprint. You are one of a kind. We all have negative chatter in our minds. We all have doubt and fear. You need to push past them because the world needs you. What are some things you need to stop telling yourself? (Ex: I'm not good enough).

_____

_____

_____

_____

_____

_____

_____

_____

_____

7 QUEENDOM TIP

Don't be afraid of your power. Own it. Don't allow anyone to make you feel small. You got this. Queen up!

Your Power

Queen, stand tall in your power

Do not shrink or waver or cower.

You're confident and that you should be

Don't bring your confidence down to a lesser degree.

The people who love you for who you are

Are rooting for you to rise as a star.

Don't dim your light to appease

There's no one that you actually have to please.

Haters, they come and they go

Don't allow them to steal your world show.

You are the one in control

Don't let anyone tamper with your soul.

Queen, don't apologize for your power

Everyone can't handle Queenly super power.

7 QUEENDOM REFLECTION

Queen up! Own that queen in you. Stop letting people's opinions dictate what you do and don't do. Continue to believe in yourself and own your power. How are you going to show up in the world from now on?

_____

_____

_____

_____

_____

_____

_____

_____

_____

8 QUEENDOM TIP

Love yourself first before you love someone else.

Queenness

There comes a time

When you must demand

That your Queenness and self worth

Will not be defined by a man.

Society would have you think

That being single is a disease

The truth is, that's a lie

But it's up to you what you choose to believe.

See, when you know who you are

You don't really worry about what people have to say

You continue to live your life

Live life on your terms in your own way.

Queen, you are a diamond

You are regal, a precious jewel

Any man that would think to degrade you

Would have to be a damn fool.

You are a child of God

You are God's daughter, a gem that is rare

No matter what tried to break you

You are unique, no one can compare.

Be the Queen that you are

You are royalty at its best

Don't settle for less than you deserve

Because Queens never settle for less.

8 QUEENDOM REFLECTION

Queen, you are not defined by your relationship status. Your value as a woman is not defined by whether or not you're married! Feel free to take some time out for yourself and stay single. Focus on self-care and self-love. If you want to be in a relationship, that's great. But never believe that you are anything less than the Queen that you are if you're not in a relationship. Love and take care of you FIRST. Do something you've been wanting to do but have been afraid to or just told yourself that you couldn't find the time. Write it out below.

_____

_____

_____

_____

_____

_____

_____

_____

9 QUEENDOM TIP

Think highly of yourself. You're a Queen. If you think lowly of yourself, people will treat you that way. Increase your self-love and maintain a positive perception of yourself. You are worthy.

<u>Queen (Parts of Speech poem)</u>

A Queen,

  Royal and Immaculate,

    Educates and Empowers,

      Perfectly,

        Herself.

9 QUEENDOM REFLECTION

You are a Queen. What you think of yourself is important. How do you honestly perceive yourself?

_____

_____

_____

_____

_____

_____

_____

_____

10 QUEENDOM TIP

You shouldn't have to give up your goals and dreams to be with someone.
You deserve to be with someone who supports them.

<u>Grinding Queens (5 W's poem)</u>

We

Grind for our dreams

Everyday

Across the globe

To honor our God-given gifts.

10 QUEENDOM REFLECTION

The right person will complement you. They will support you. They will be an addition, not a subtraction. What is something you refuse to settle for with your next partner?

_____

_____

_____

_____

_____

_____

_____

_____

11 QUEENDOM TIP

Don't let someone's limited thinking stop you. Anything your mind can conceive you can achieve.

A Queen (Cinquain poem)

A Queen

Is confident

She believes in herself

She expects the best and trusts God

Winner.

11 QUEENDOM REFLECTION

Always believe in yourself. What is something you can do to remind yourself of how great you are?

_____
_____
_____
_____
_____
_____
_____
_____

12 QUEENDOM TIP

A man that is looking for his queen wouldn't want her to settle for less than the best (a King like him). So keep your standards Queens.

A Relationship

Queen, do not be mistaken

A relationship should bring out your best

The man that you wanna give your heart to

Shouldn't be a man that minimizes your zest.

You are a woman of high value

Your man should have the qualities of a king

He shouldn't be getting all of the benefits

Of a wife, when he hasn't given you a ring.

No, you are not being too demanding

To expect to be treated like a Queen

No, you don't have to lower your standards

Having high self-esteem does not make you a woman that's mean.

A man that is looking for his Queen

Wouldn't want you to take less than the best

He's coming to love you unconditionally

And put all your worries and past pain to rest.

He'll love you for your bare naked soul

As your King, he'll be happy to fill this role.

12 QUEENDOM REFLECTION

Kings desire Queens. A King wants a Queen that is confident in whom she is. For the right person, you don't have to minimize any aspect of you. A Queen has standards and doesn't relinquish them for anyone. What are some qualities you desire in your King?

_____

_____

_____

_____

_____

_____

_____

_____

13 QUEENDOM TIP

People make priorities for the things they want to make a priority.
Relationships are no different. You don't have to prove you're worthy of
his time. He's just not the right one.

<u>Woman (Parts of Speech poem)</u>

A Woman,

Feminine and Regal,

Nurtures and Inspires,

Phenomenally,

Herself.

13 QUEENDOM REFLECTION

If the man is interested, it will show in his actions towards you. You don't have to chase him. Instead of focusing on him, focus on you. What is something you can do to better yourself?

_____

_____

_____

_____

_____

_____

_____

_____

14 QUEENDOM TIP

If you want better friends, get rid of the toxic ones. If you want better furniture, get rid of the old furniture. Make space for what you're asking for. New things can't come to you if there's no room for them.

Dream House (Cinquain poem)

Dream House

Visualize

It is waiting on you

You are worthy of your dream house

It's yours.

14 QUEENDOM REFLECTION

Have you done your spring cleaning? It may not be spring but the concept remains the same. You can't expect new and better things when you keep clinging onto the old stuff. That stuff can include old habits, old negative thoughts that don't serve you, old clothes, etc. What is something you need to get rid of to make room for something better?

_____
_____
_____
_____
_____
_____
_____
_____

15 QUEENDOM TIP

Do not minimize who you are to appease anyone. Your vision is your vision. God gave it to you. Your dreams are your dreams. Stop letting other people dictate how you choose to live your life. You're a Queen. Enough said.

<u>Your Life (Cinquain poem)</u>

Your life

Is a blessing

It matters, you matter

Pursue your dreams and your purpose

Divine.

15 QUEENDOM REFLECTION

It's never too late to pursue your goals and dreams. What is something you've always dreamt of doing?

_____

_____

_____

_____

_____

_____

_____

_____

16 QUEENDOM TIP

You cannot live a brave life without disappointing some people and it's okay. The people who care for you, who are really rooting for your rise, will not be disappointed. The only people who are disappointed are the ones who have their own agenda. ~Oprah Winfrey

Be Selfish

Queen, it's time to be selfish

It's time to take care of your needs

It's time to make you a priority

To get back to your goals and your dreams.

It's not selfish to do things in your best interest

You've been programmed to put yourself last

It's time for you to put yourself first

Without explaining yourself to anyone that asks.

Be selfish to get to your next level

You deserve to be happy and fulfilled

You deserve to share your God-given talents

To live a life full of fun with many thrills.

Queen, it's your right to be selfish

Prioritize your wants and your needs

No more of your desires on the back burner

Being your authentic self is what the world needs.

16 QUEENDOM REFLECTION

You don't owe anyone an apology for going after your goals and dreams. You don't have to apologize for who you are. God has given all of us different gifts and talents. And to be all that you can be and should be, there's no way that you can please everyone. You may have to be selfish with your time and energy to get to your next level. There's nothing wrong with that. What is something you will stop tolerating from people?

_____
_____
_____
_____
_____
_____
_____
_____

17 QUEENDOM TIP

Put yourself first and take care of yourself so you attract better.
Desperation is dangerous. Having low standards or no standards attracts
low quality men.

__Desperation__

Queen, make sure you are certain

That a relationship is actually what you need

It's not queen-like to do it out of desperation

No matter how lonely it may be.

You are way too significant

To settle for less than the best

If you're using him just to fill a void

Then you're no different than a woman accepting less.

A relationship should be an enhancer

Not something you get into cause you're bored

Make sure your intention is genuine

Because a King sees a Queen as a reward.

Increase your self-love in all areas

Enjoy your own company while you can

Take time out for you and be selfish

Live it up and be happy first without a man.

Queen, make sure you're not desperate

Be patient and wait on God's best

Don't compromise who you are or your standards

Because Queens never settle for less.

17 QUEENDOM REFLECTION

Queens aren't desperate. They understand their value and will wait as long as needed for the RIGHT King. Are you willing to wait for the best or settle for less and why?

_____

_____

_____

_____

_____

_____

_____

_____

18 QUEENDOM TIP

Love yourself enough to wait for the right person rather than rush to get married, especially if you know in your gut that it's not right.

<u>Lady (Parts of Speech poem)</u>

A Lady,

Classy and Sophisticated,

Radiates and Astonishes,

Phenomenally,

Herself.

18 QUEENDOM REFLECTION

Queens are not in a rush to have somebody just for the sake of having somebody. They love themselves and honor themselves. Is it important to you to have the right person in your life or will just anybody do?

_____

_____

_____

_____

_____

_____

_____

_____

19 QUEENDOM TIP

You are far too special not to be a priority in someone's life. Never dishonor yourself.

<u>Mistress</u>

Queen, there's no honor in being a side piece

You're in jeopardy of losing your crown

Your integrity is being called into question

Your empire being brought down to the ground.

I can't understand why you'd settle

You're sacred from your head to your toes

How dare you be okay with such lowness

When there's a man that wants to worship you and your soul.

This comes from a place of love and not judgment

Don't get defensive when my concern is your heart

Real Queens look out for one another

Instead of competing and tearing each other apart.

You're more than a man's play toy, you're a person

You are God's daughter with a soul that needs to be fed

It's time for you to reclaim your Queenly power

No more being mistress, that relationship is already dead.

Queen, you must get rid of that lowlife

You're worthy of being in first place

Don't settle for being an option and not a priority

A man like that can easily be replaced.

Queen, work on you and increase your confidence

Love yourself so there's never another time

Where you settle for such crap and lowly behavior

Never again, you can return to your Queendom at any time.

19 QUEENDOM REFLECTION

Despite what you may see on TV, there's nothing Queenly about being a side chick/mistress knowingly. You're royalty. You don't have to settle for 2nd best. You deserve to be a priority, #1. What advice would you give to a woman who is currently a mistress or is thinking about being one?

_____

_____

_____

_____

_____

_____

_____

_____

20 QUEENDOM TIP

You're royalty. Act like it.

Royalty (Parts of Speech poem)

The Royalty,

Striking and Majestic,

Gleams and Magnifies,

Powerfully,

Itself.

20 QUEENDOM REFLECTION

Embrace the Queen that you are. What does it mean to you to be royalty?

_____

_____

_____

_____

_____

_____

_____

_____

21 QUEENDOM TIP

Stand firm in Queenness at your workplace. Your crown is still in effect.

<u>Your Salary</u>

Queen, you have been programmed

To settle for less than the best

They want you to be happy with bread crumbs

But it's time to put that sh*t to rest.

A Queen has a standard of excellence

Her highness is the level of elite

So when it comes to salary negotiations

You better command the salary that they need to meet.

Queen, stop sitting there all quiet

When you know that promotion should've been yours

Speak up and make them recognize your high value

Kindly tell them, next time, you will walk out the door.

Queen, stop settling for the lowest salaries

You are smart with a myriad of skills

Make sure you command an amount for your real value

As a Queen, you more than fit the bill.

Queen, you are not to be taken for granted

Remind people that you are not the one

You will not tolerate any bad or negative treatment

Stand your ground, stand up for yourself for once.

21 QUEENDOM REFLECTION

Your Queen status doesn't change just because you punch a clock. Remember who you are. You don't have to accept the bare minimum if you know and believe you're worth more. Did you negotiate your salary/contract in your current position or just accept what was given to you and why?

_____

_____

_____

_____

_____

_____

_____

_____

22 QUEENDOM TIP

You're enough, Queen. You never know who you're inspiring. Keep moving forward.

Queen (5 W's poem)

A phenomenal Queen

Ascends her Queendom throne

As she prepares for each day

On her majestic territory

To salute her fellow Queens.

22 QUEENDOM REFLECTION

There's a quote that says 'You inspire people who pretend not to even see you'. Name 1 person that you've inspired in some way no matter who they are or how old they are. How did that make you feel?

_____

_____

_____

_____

_____

_____

_____

_____

23 QUEENDOM TIP

You're a Queen. Sex with you is a privilege, an honor. Act like it.

Your Jewel (Cinquain poem)

Your jewel

A gift from God

Treat it like it's a prize

Men must prove they're worthy of it

It's gold.

23 QUEENDOM REFLECTION

You're a Queen. It's an honor to be in your presence let alone your body. Be careful of the soul ties you create. Your soul is at stake. How will you honor your body going forward?

_____

_____

_____

_____

_____

_____

_____

24 QUEENDOM TIP

Let the world see you for who you are. Honor your gifts.

<u>Your Gifts (Cinquain poem)</u>

Your gifts

Are Godly gifts

To be shared with the world

So do not deny who you are

Proudly.

24 QUEENDOM REFLECTION

Stop hiding your gifts and talents from the world. The world needs you Queen. What is one of your gifts and how can you share it?

_____

_____

_____

_____

_____

_____

_____

_____

25 QUEENDOM TIP

You deserve whatever your heart desires. Don't let the world tell you otherwise.

__Dream Car__

The way she looks, of elegance and style

Your eyes are glued to her make and model.

You dream of her more than you want to admit

You can't wait to change gears on that beautiful stick shift.

Your dream car she is, a beauty to see

And yours she will be once you change your beliefs.

You deserve your dream car but you've got to let go

Of negative beliefs and the lies you've been told.

There is nothing special that you have to do

Just visualize and believe that she was made for you.

Having your dream car, consider it done

Expect her to show up and she will come.

And once she comes, hit the road and have some fun!

25 QUEENDOM REFLECTION

You can have what you want. Don't let anyone make you feel bad for wanting more than what is considered normal or status quo. What is something you've always wanted?

_____

_____

_____

_____

_____

_____

_____

_____

26 QUEENDOM TIP

Say Yes to yourself.

<u>Say No</u>

Queen, you are entitled to happiness

At times that means you must say No

No is a word you should be using

Just advising you in case you didn't know.

Queens do not have to be saviors

We are human with issues of our own

The obligation is to help when we are able

But in no way does that mean sacrifice our throne.

People out here want to use you

Don't be fooled by their charm

They are wolves disguised in sheep cloth

So called friends and family that want to cause you harm.

So stop allowing yourself to be a target

Being kind doesn't equate to being a fool

Say No anytime that you need to

Putting yourself first must be the golden rule.

Queen, you can say No and not feel guilty

Self love is the highest love of all

You are worthy and deserving of all God's riches

Taking care of you is the proper protocol.

26 QUEENDOM REFLECTION

We as women are conditioned to put others before ourselves. Queen, there's nothing wrong with helping others but it shouldn't be at the expense of your happiness. In other words, you helping shouldn't put you in a bad position. Sometimes you need to say No. By saying No, you are saying Yes to yourself. When is the last time you actually said Yes to yourself and did something nice for yourself?

_____

_____

_____

_____

_____

_____

_____

_____

27 QUEENDOM TIP

Your clothes speak. Make sure they're speaking your language. Looking fabulous is merely a reflection of feeling fabulous on the inside.
~Dr. Carol Parker Walsh

<u>Attire</u>

Queen, your wardrobe speaks volumes

Be sure it represents who you are

You are not defined by your clothes

But as a Queen, you should still dress the part.

Nothing that you wear should be broken

Meaning holey or torn in any way

Nothing in your wardrobe should be damaged

You're a Queen, that's a significant role you play.

What you wear has an effect on your confidence

What you wear can affect how you feel

So when you wear things that aren't of your character

It can cause you to miss out on the perfect deal.

Queen, show up in your elegance

Dress accordingly and show others how it's done

Have dignity and flaunt your individuality

You're a Queen, you've already won.

27 QUEENDOM REFLECTION

Your clothes affect how you feel. You should wear clothes that represent the Queen you are. How do you feel on a daily basis based on your wardrobe?

_____

_____

_____

_____

_____

_____

_____

_____

28 QUEENDOM TIP

Start before you're ready. Build the plane as you fly. You got this, Queen.

Your Business

Queen, your vision is your vision

Your dreams are your dreams just for you

Stop letting people who have given up on their own dreams

Negatively affect and dictate what you do.

Start your business, you know that it's inside you

Have faith that God will see you through

God gave you your gifts for a reason

It's up to you what you actually choose to do.

Start your business, your fans are still waiting

Start your business, there's no time to delay

Trust that you will have everything that you need

And whenever you have doubt, just take time to pray.

I believe in you Queen and your possibilities

I'm with you in spirit as your sister and fellow Queen

Please don't live a life without your purpose

Believe in yourself and the fulfillment of your dreams.

28 QUEENDOM REFLECTION

You don't have to have it all figured out Queen. Just take it one step at a time. There's a business inside of you, a product, an idea, something that the world needs. What is stopping you from taking action?

_____

_____

_____

_____

_____

_____

_____

_____

29 QUEENDOM TIP

You're a gift from God. Never forget that.

Toot Your Horn

A great thing happened

When God created Eve

This woman – a work of art

An image of beauty, so serene.

Women are the backbone

We are powerful and strong

We know how to keep the family together

If anything ever goes wrong.

We are beautiful in so many ways

We are perfect in our bare form

We know how to handle any storms

And if necessary, we can conform.

A woman is a gift from God

She is something man can't live without

She is a diamond to be cherished

One of the greatest creations without a doubt.

We must celebrate our women

For all of the wonderful things that they do

Because the truth of the matter is

Without women, things wouldn't run smooth.

We are women of value

We are unique, there is no other

We have so much light to give to the world

So we must love and support one another.

God created Eve

And a masterpiece was born

The world has never been the same

So ladies, remember to toot your horn!

29 QUEENDOM REFLECTION

You're a blessing to the world Queen. Please know, believe and remember that. Stop being so hard on yourself and give yourself some credit. What is one thing you're going to do to celebrate yourself?

_____
_____
_____
_____
_____
_____
_____
_____

30 QUEENDOM TIP

Every day is a new day. Don't let your past dictate your future. Who you are today and who you are becoming is what matters. Walk with your head high. Rise up as the Queen you are.

<u>Masterpiece</u>

I know we've been programmed

To always fear the unknown

I know most of us have gifts and talents

That have yet to be shown.

I know sometimes you wonder

Why you're here, why you were born

I know many of us have been through so much

Some of us fall in the category of a woman scorned.

When you look into the mirror

You are disappointed with what you see

You cry and tear yourself down

Sometimes disgusted, you ask yourself, what happened to me?

You've been broken, hurt, and abused

After you trusted those closest to you.

The stories are all the same

No matter your color, gender or race

Ladies, it's time to reclaim your value

It's time to click erase.

Everyone goes through struggle

Everyone experiences strife

What doesn't kill you only makes you stronger

Trust and believe, no one has a perfect life.

Learn to forgive those that hurt you

So you can take back your power

Let the past go and start to move forward

No more drowning in sorrow or cower.

You are a beautiful child of God

No matter your past mistakes

Have faith that it will all work out

With God's help, you will never break.

You are strong, loving and kind

You are blessed and don't forget fine.

There is nothing you can't do

But first you have to believe

Believe in yourself and know you are worthy

You are the chief of your magnificent dreams.

Take a stand for who you are

Stand in your truth and be in peace

No more bondage, no more limiting beliefs

Just walking tall, head up with ease.

You are not tainted, you are a masterpiece.

30 QUEENDOM REFLECTION

Today marks the end of you settling Queen. You are a gift from God, an absolute Masterpiece. We get what we tolerate. Only you hold the key to the manifestations of your hearts desires. You are worthy and deserving of it all. You are a Queen and will always be a Queen. You are royalty. Now... What are you going to do differently?

_____

_____

_____

_____

_____

_____

_____

_____

_____

ABOUT THE AUTHOR

Radesha "Desh" Dixon is an author, poet, model and pageant titleholder. She is also the author of No More Broken Records: 5 Tips To Change Your Tune and Transform Your Life, available on Amazon. She is the Creator and Founder of No More Broken Records™, a movement to empower women not to settle; To stop the repeated cycles like a broken record. She believes it's never too late to make positive changes in your life.

She is available for motivational speaking and poetry.

Connect with her on social media.

Facebook: https://www.facebook.com/petitewithpurpose
https://www.facebook.com/nomorebrokenrecords/

Instagram: https://www.instagram.com/deshdixon/
https://www.instagram.com/nomorebrokenrecords/

Website: https://www.queensdontsettle.com

Podcast: https://anchor.fm/desh-dixon/

I'd Love Your Feedback!

Reviews are extremely important to authors. If you've enjoyed this book, I'd really appreciate if you'd consider leaving me one. It will help me to share my work with more fabulous women like you!

Thank you so much!

And don't forget –

You're a Queen. Queens Don't Settle….

Queen Desh

Made in the USA
Middletown, DE
26 May 2021